STRAVINSKY
Op.7 No.2

ETUDE

For
Piano Solo

Belwin Mills Publishing Corp.
MELVILLE, N. Y. 11747
PRINTED IN U S A

II.

I. STRAWINSKY. Op. 7.

Allegro brillante. M.M. ♩.=76.

mf
p
cre _ scen _ do
al
ff
3997

mf
p
mf
pp
cre scendo poco a poco
8
8
8

p
sempre stacc.
poco più f
f
8
mf

sf mf
sf mf
sf mf
cre _ secendo poco a
poco
dim. assai
p poco a poco
cre _ scen _ do
sf sf sf ff